MW01680803

Blessings on your Journey

Babs 2023

The Address to Your Heart

BY BABS FEE

Illustrations by Ara Elizabeth Schmidt

ISBN 13: 978-1-63489-040-3

Library of Congress Catalog Number: 2016940176
Printed in the United States of America
First Printing: 2016
20 19 18 17 16 5 4 3 2 1

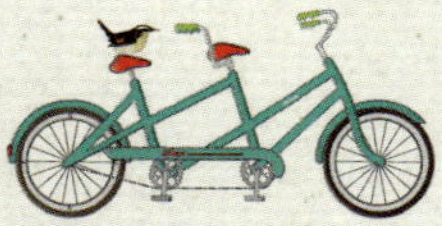

Illustrations by Ara Elizabeth Schmidt
Cover and interior design by Emily Rodvold

WISE Ink
CREATIVE ★ PUBLISHING

Wise Ink Creative Publishing
837 Glenwood Avenue
Minneapolis, MN 55405
wiseinkpub.com

To order, visit allthingswren.com. Reseller discounts available.

A portion of the proceeds will go to mental health services for US veterans.

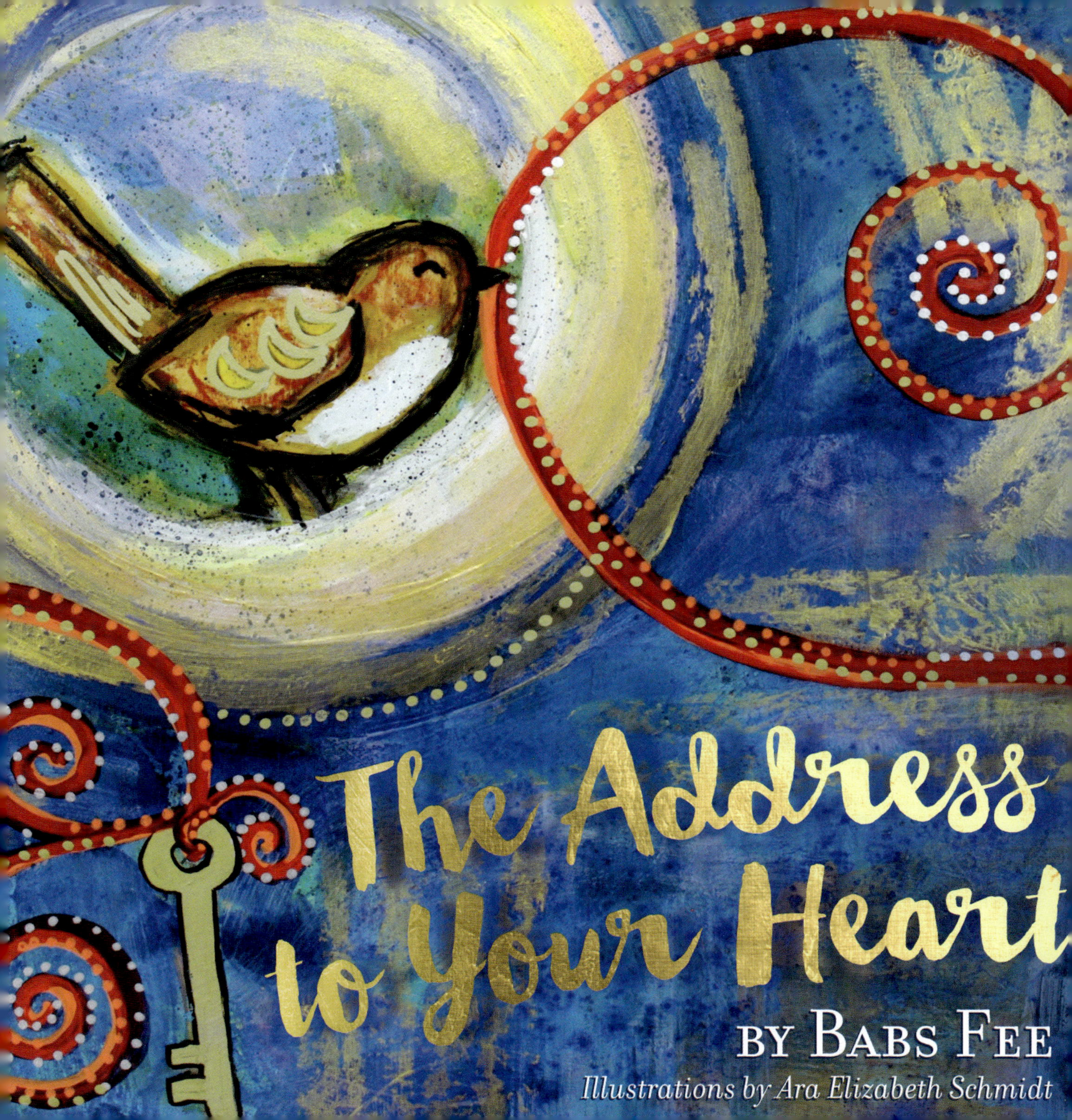
The Address to Your Heart
BY BABS FEE
Illustrations by Ara Elizabeth Schmidt

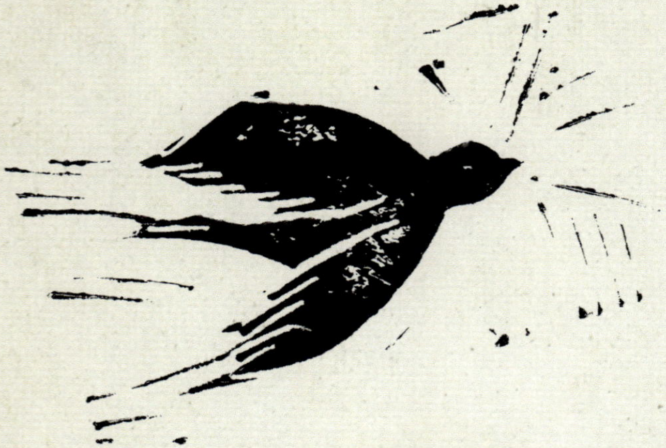

This book will benefit US veterans and help provide affordable, compassion-driven, integrative mental health treatments and healing. For updates on current developments, please follow us on **allthingswren.com**.

To six little birds, my grandchildren,
who always sing me home:
A, I, J, P, A, A, and to the sweet ones yet to be hatched.

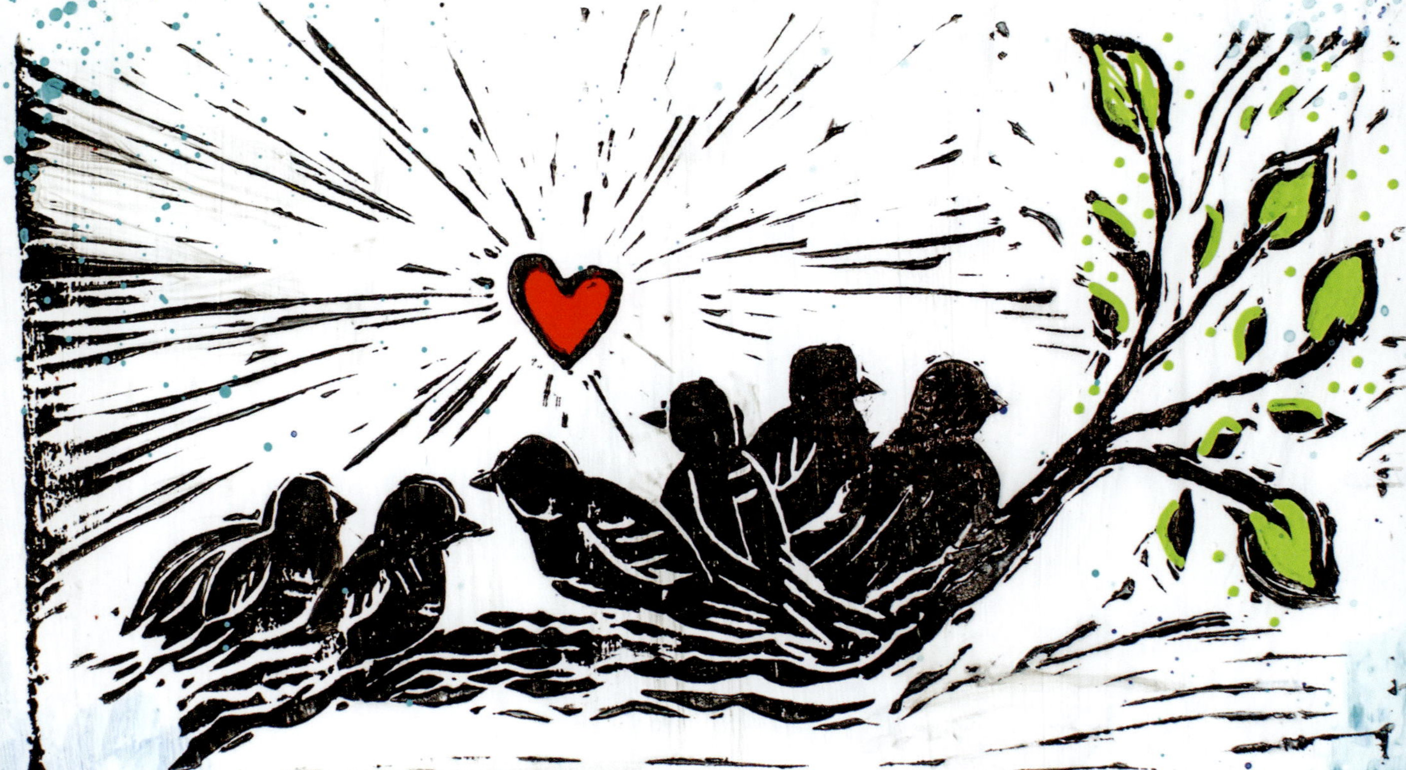

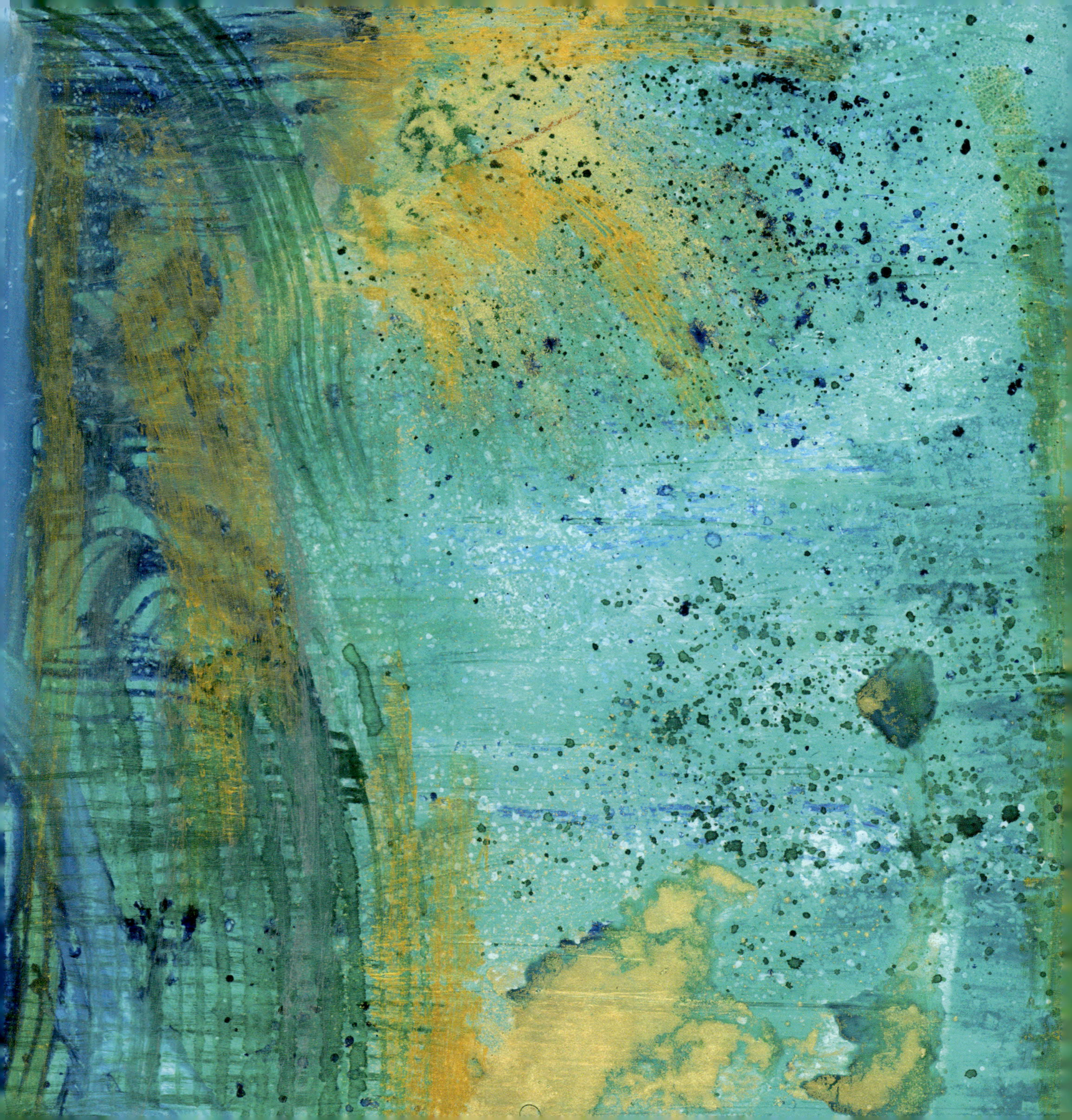

Dear Reader,

I hope this day finds you curious, wondering, and eagerly waiting.

The words in this book originated as a love letter I wrote to myself—my true self, the self I had unconsciously silenced for far too long. I knew it was time to return to my heart's home. As I quieted myself and trusted my internal compass, the words came. I listened and was led on a beautiful yet sometimes difficult journey.

I thought the words came to me simply to teach me. But, what I found was that the words came to help me remember something I had forgotten. When I opened the door to my heart, everything was just as I had left it—there I was, my true self, my most familiar. How could I have kept her quiet for so long? Why had I ever left my heart's home? To make sure this was a place I'd never lose sight of again, I gave my heart's home an address.

This book will lead you on a journey to visit your heart's home. The address to your heart is a special location, unique to you. The questions at the end of the book will help you to know your heart's address so you may never lose sight of your true self. Your address may change as your life changes, but your true self inside will always be there to guide you.

Blessings to you on your journey, and—should you find yourself nearby—you are always welcome to stop by 218 Three Moon Lane.

Love,
Babs Fee

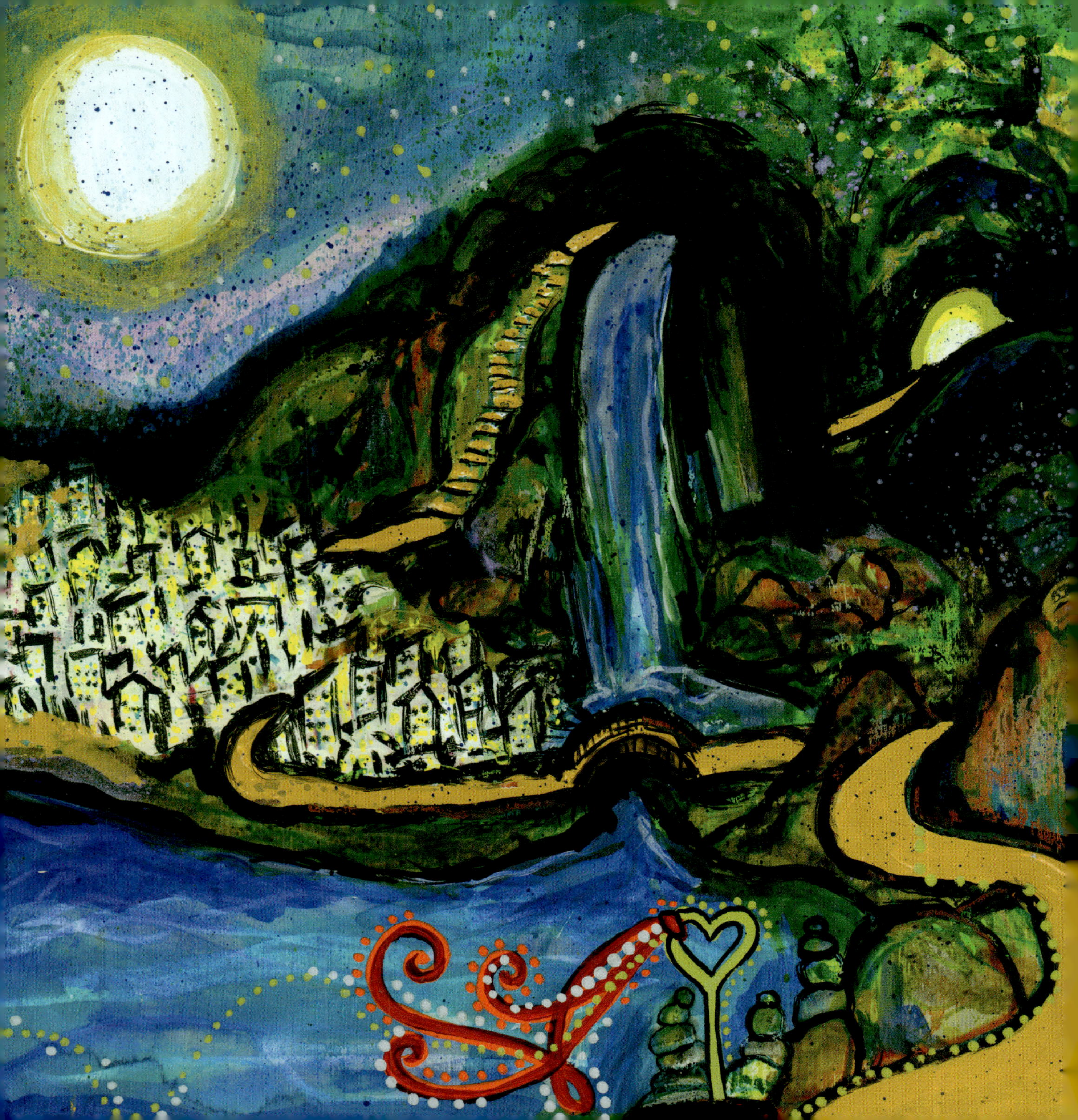

Your journey awaits
as your heart calls you home—
no need for a map,
just let yourself roam.

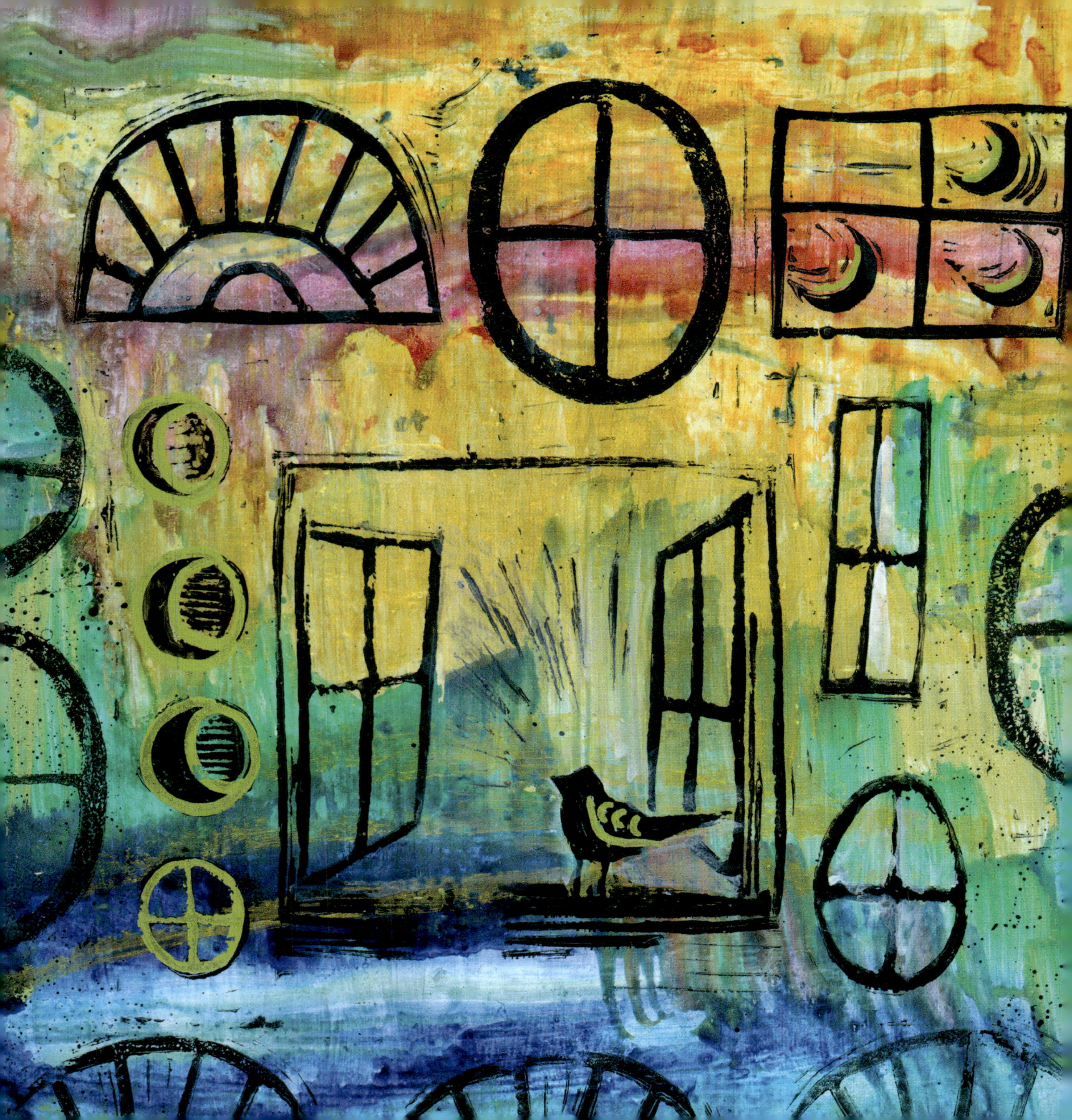

A sign may tell you it's time to go, and when that time comes, you will know.

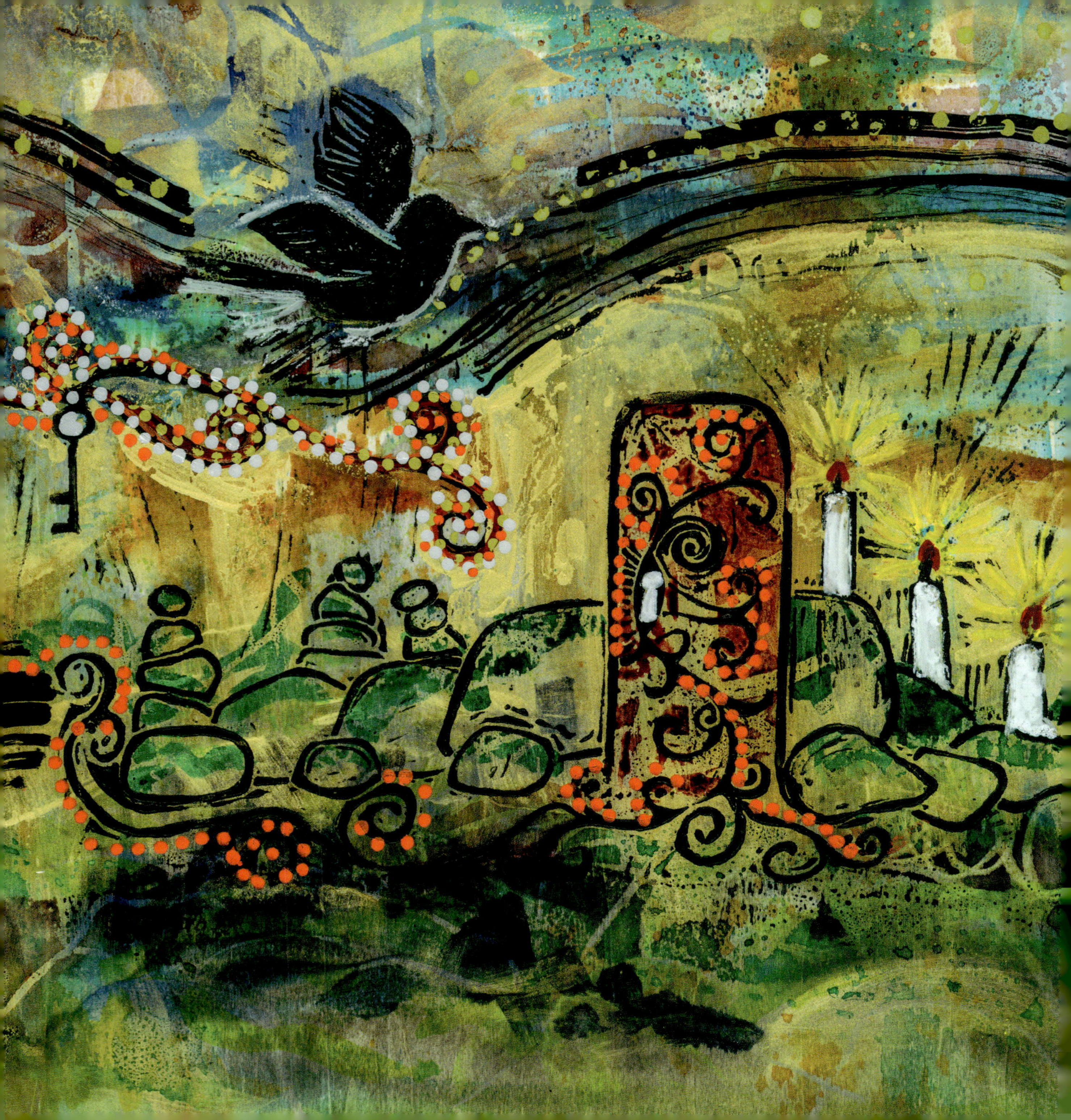

Maybe a small wren
will lead you there,
lovingly guiding you
from the air.
She stops at a door
for you to unlock;
the key's in your pocket—
there's no need to knock.

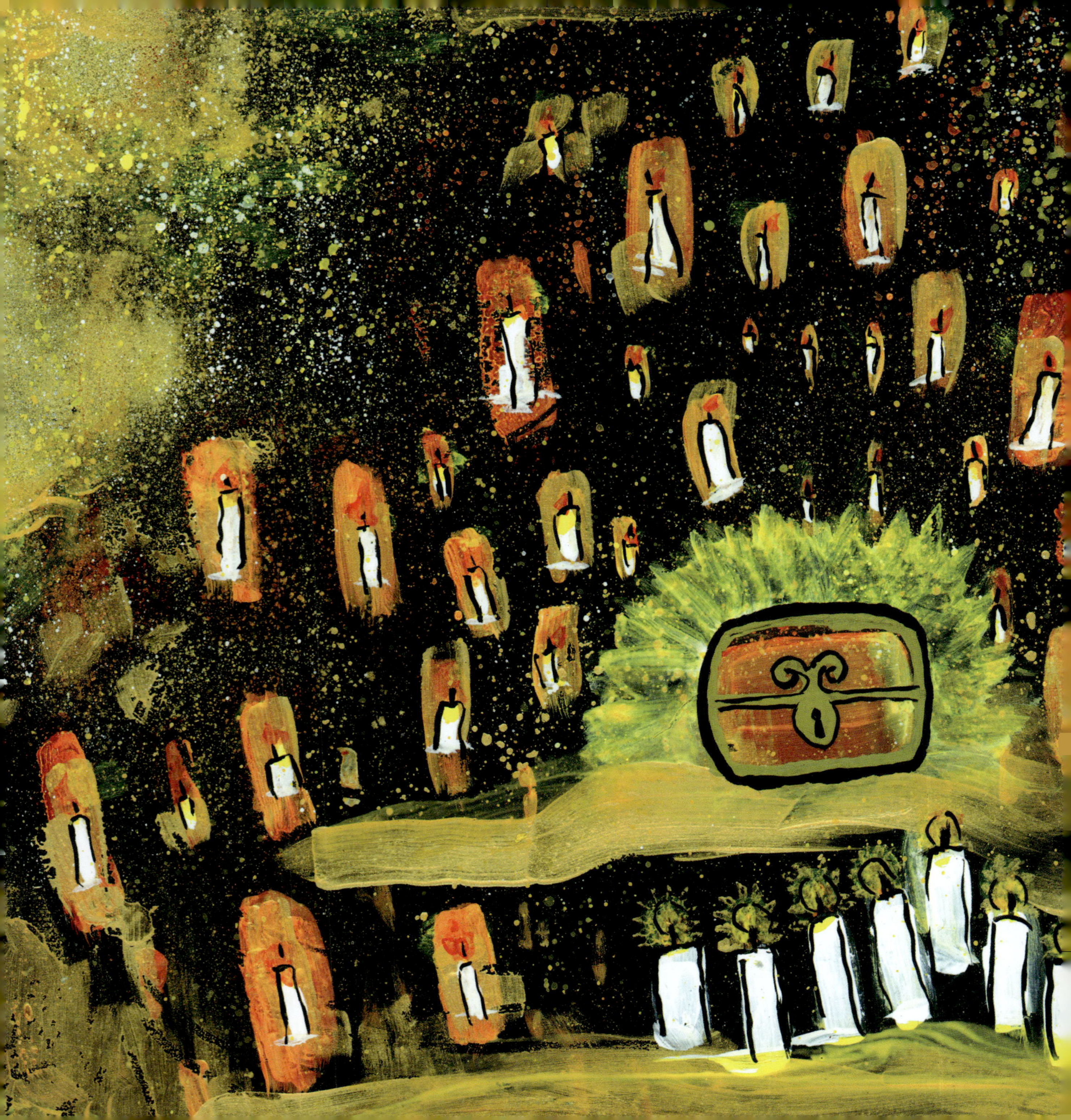

Once inside,
see the box on the shelf?
If you open it,
you'll find your true self.
This is a gift from your Creator;
in all the world, there is nothing
greater.

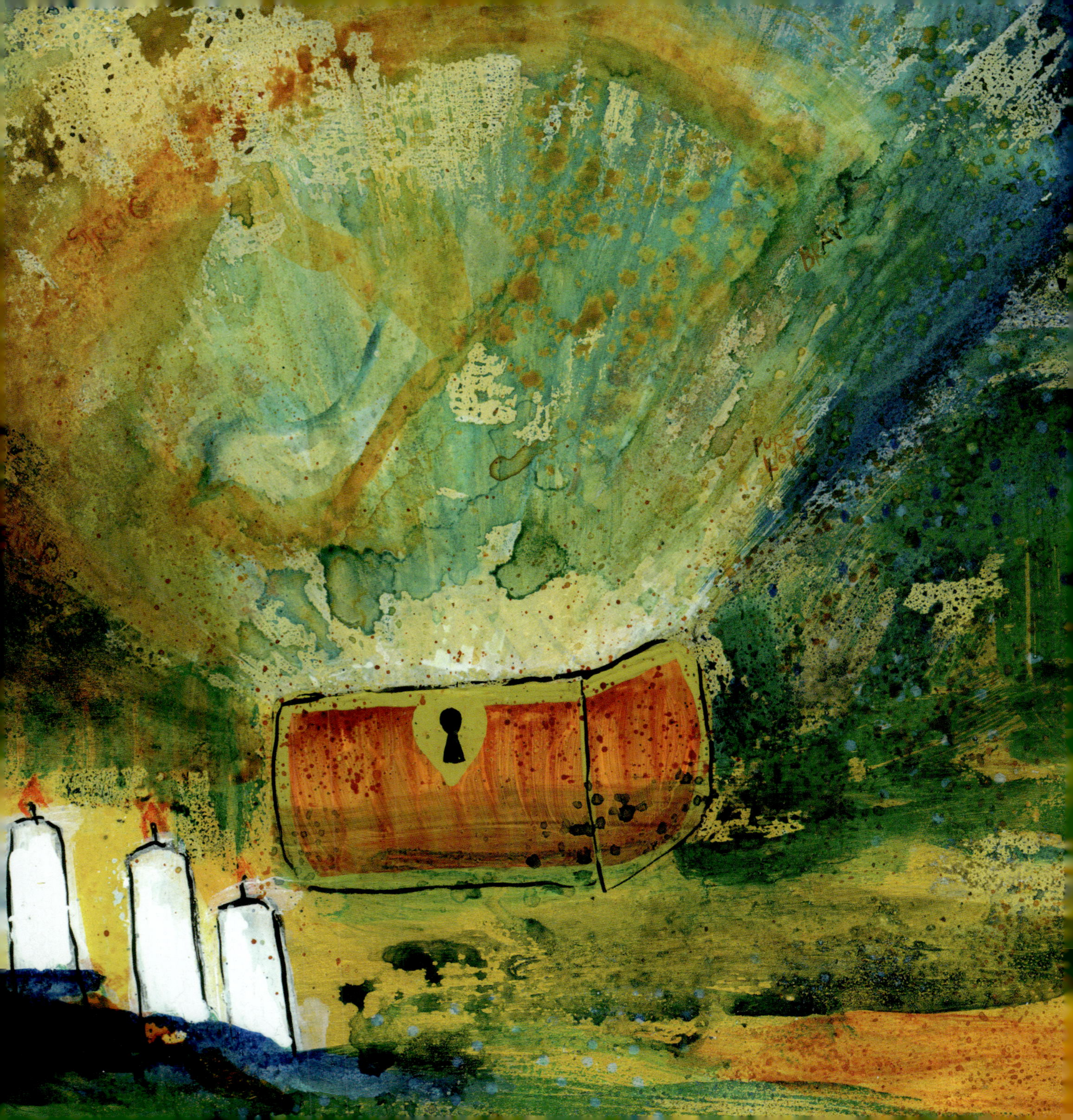
STRONG
PURE LOVE

When you open the box, stay very near,
for it has a message you must hear.
Listen closely as you close your eyes;
the words you hear are infinite and wise.
Because these words are filled with love,
you know they're from the One above.

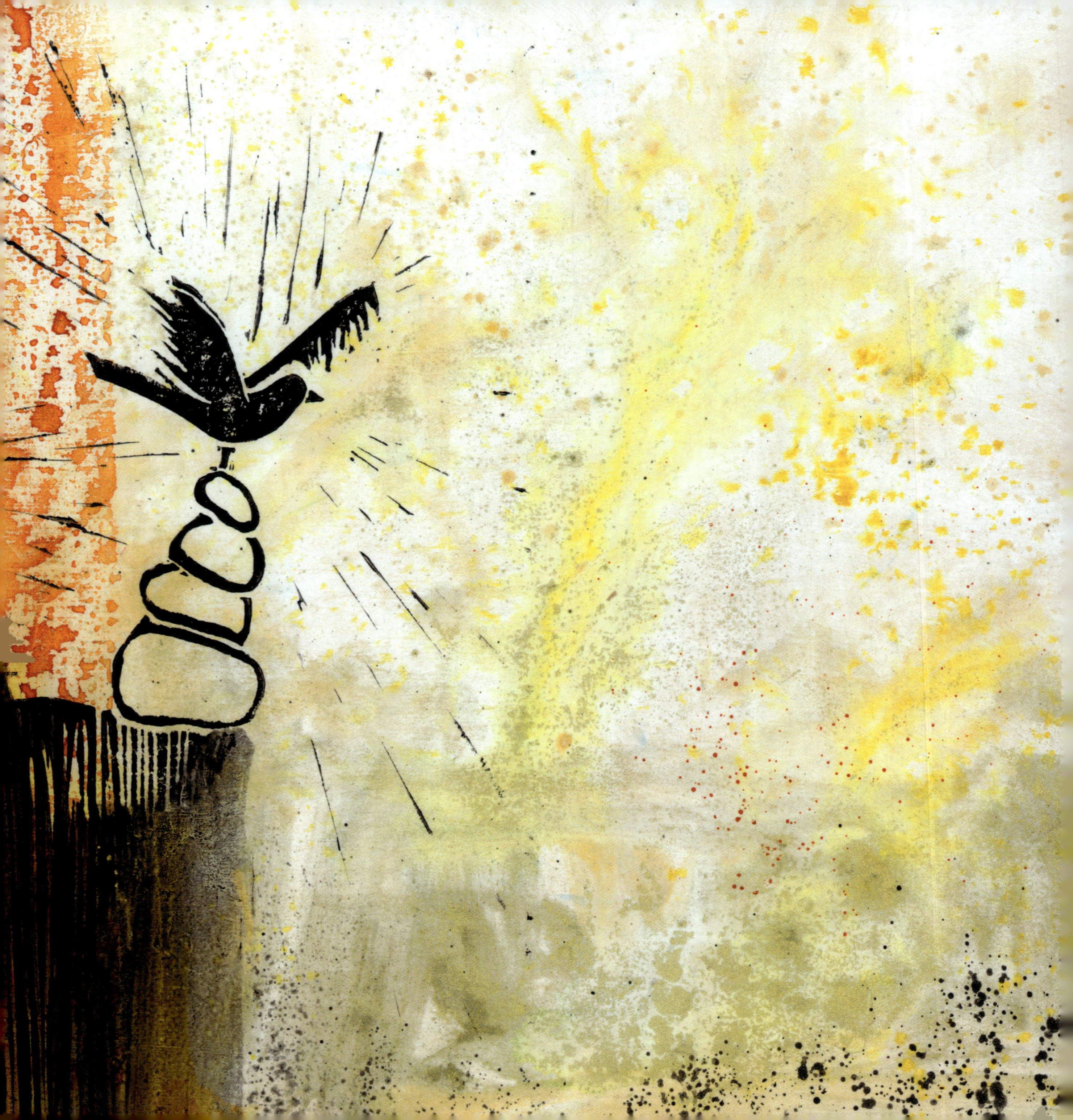

Yearning and trust
have brought you here;
now, standing alone,
you have no fear.

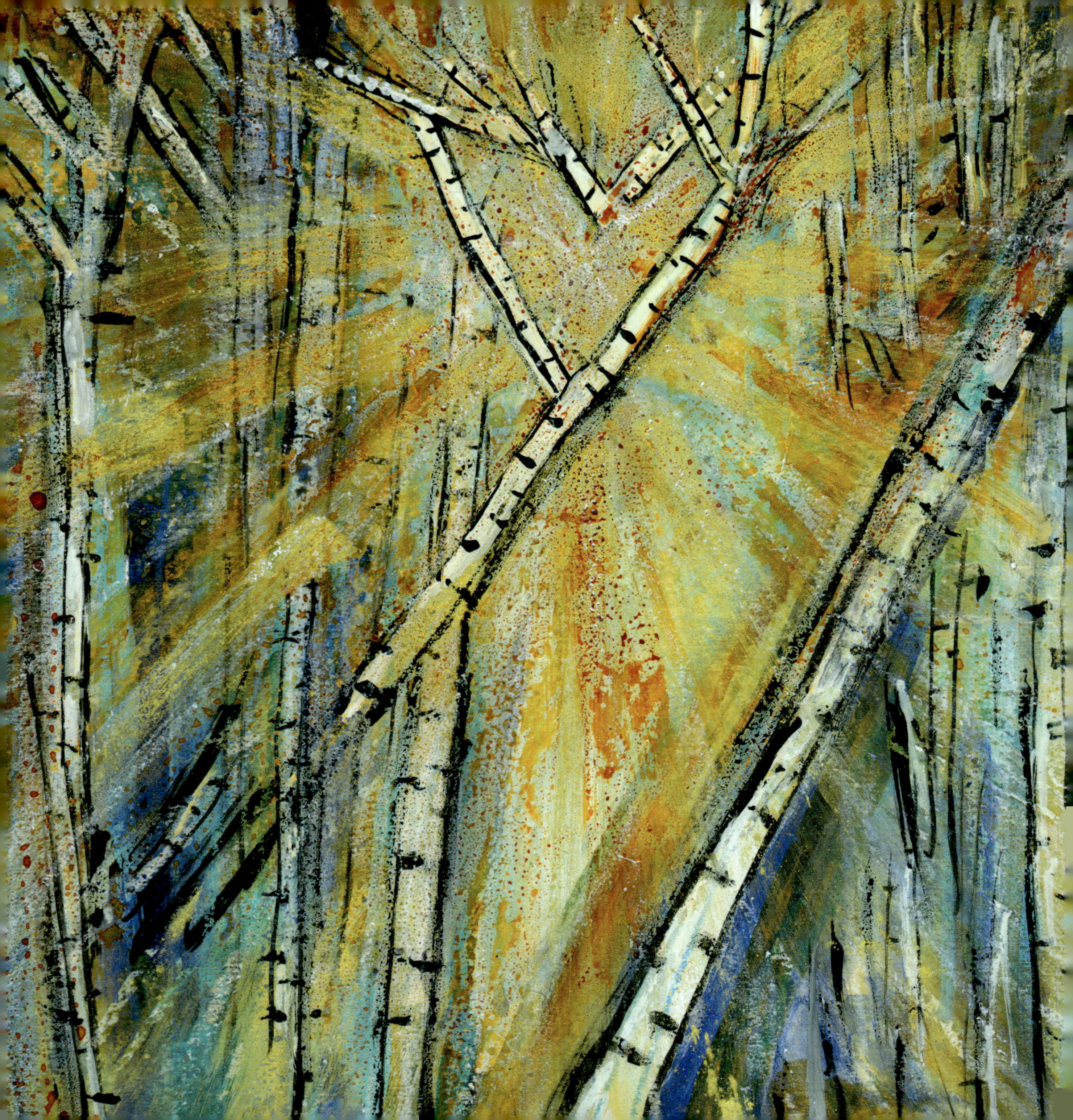

Your wisdom speaks,
you know it is true,
the bright light that's shining
is coming from you.

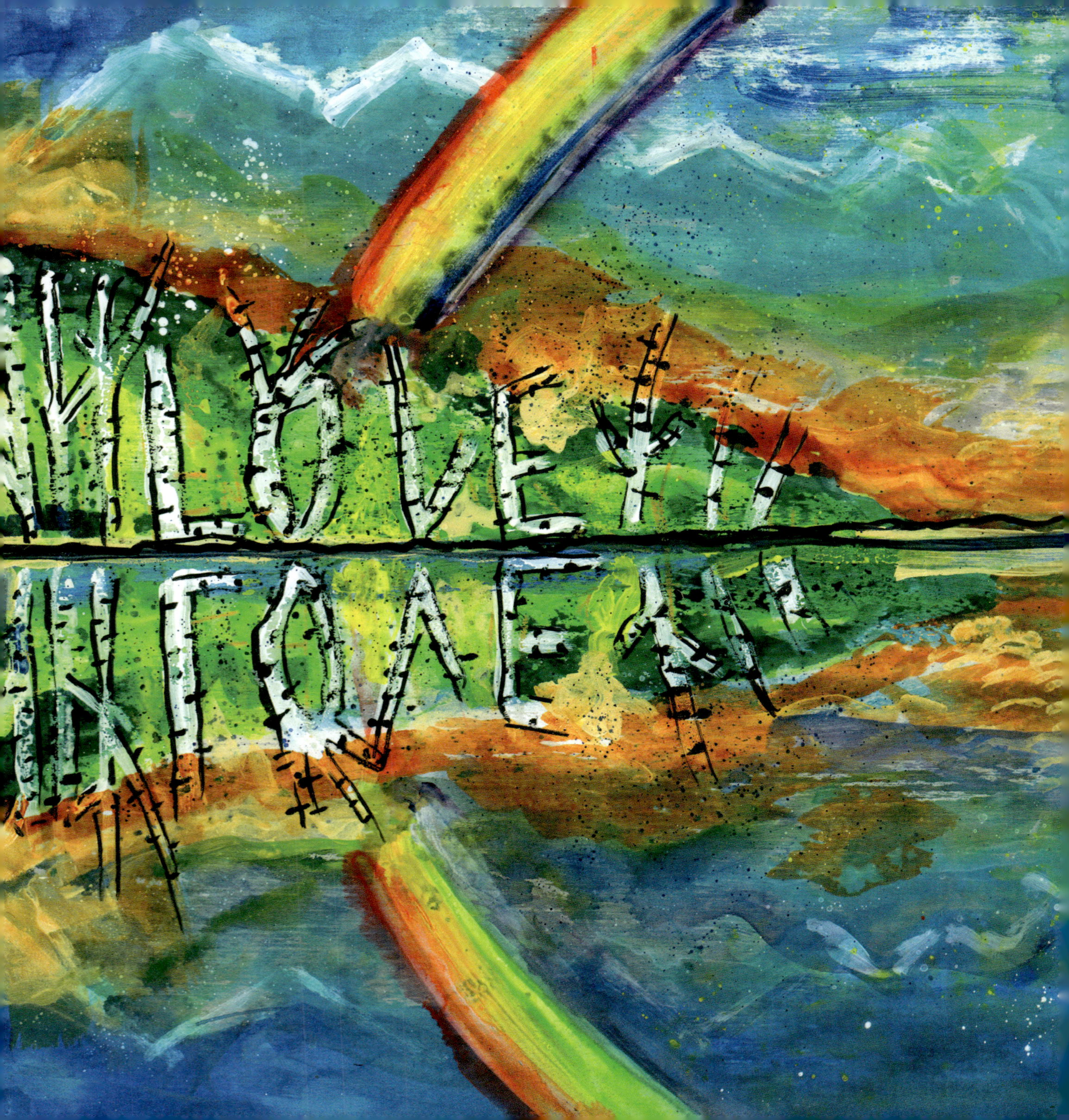
LOVE

Finally, now, you can see,
the person you are meant to be.

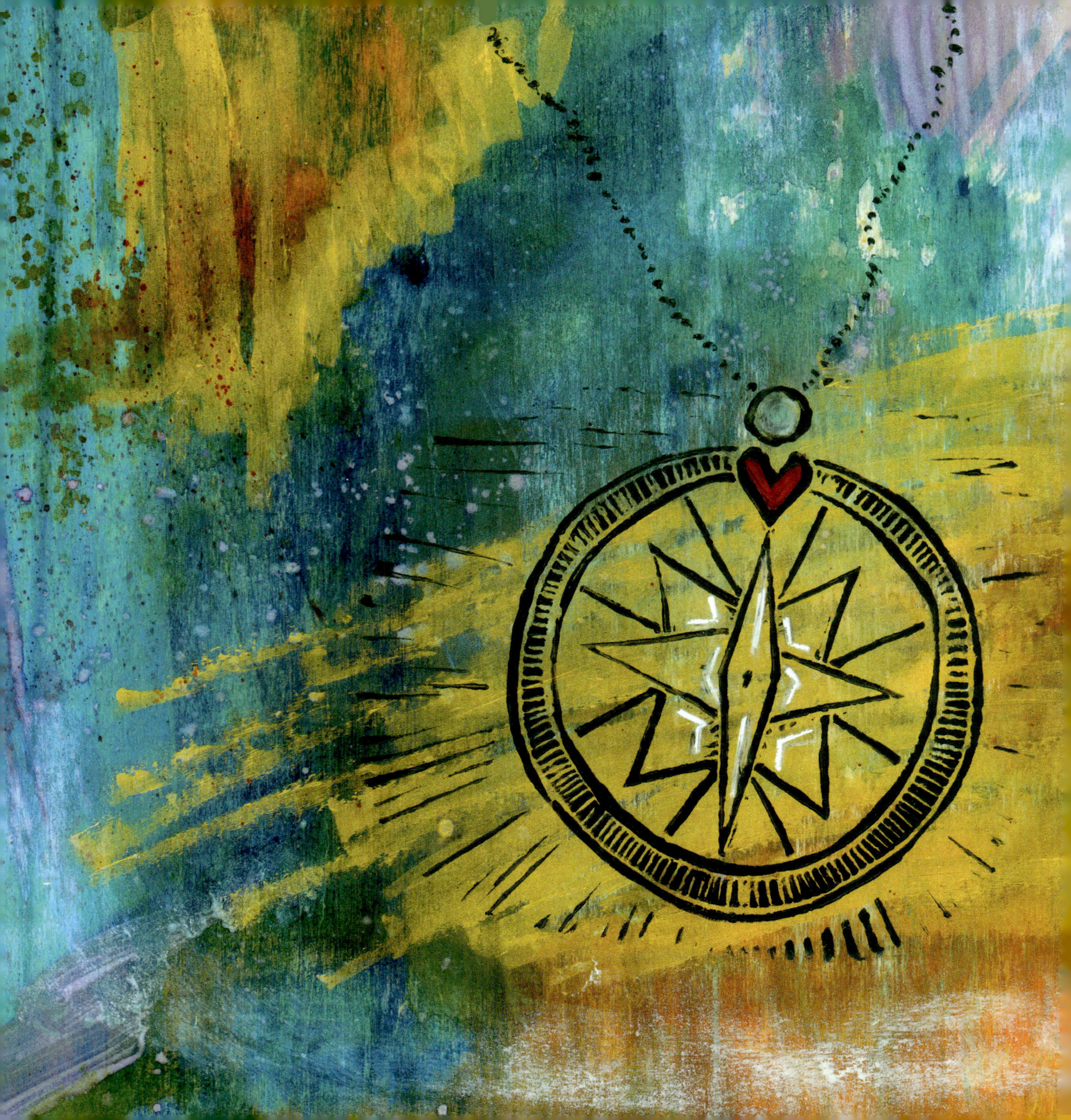

Your internal compass
led you to this place,
and here you stand in holy space.
This sacred place
is your heart's home—
it needs an address of its own.

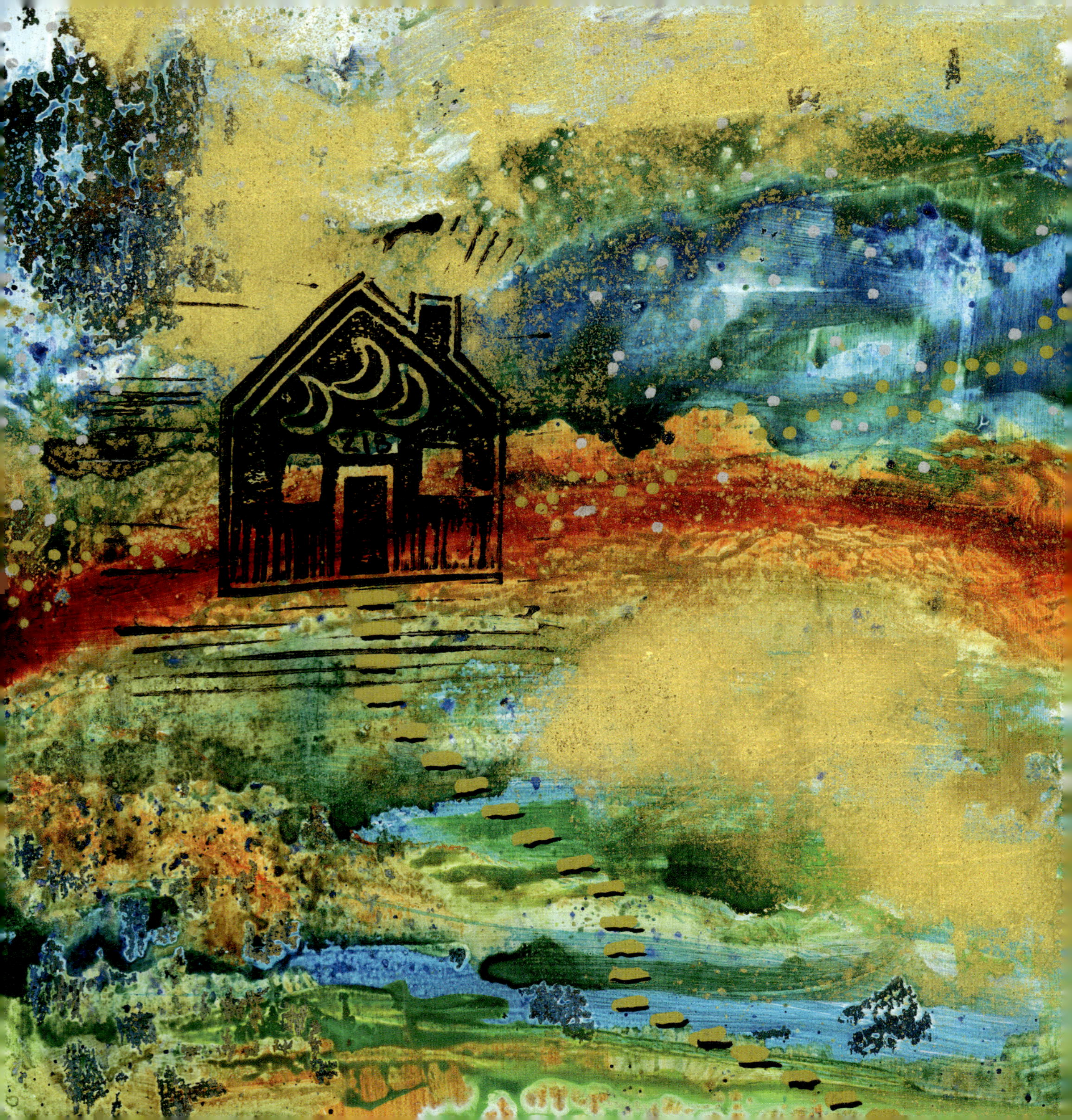

So, name the place—
it's your creation,
from a dream or your
imagination.
Like 218 Three Moon Lane,
no one's address will be the same.

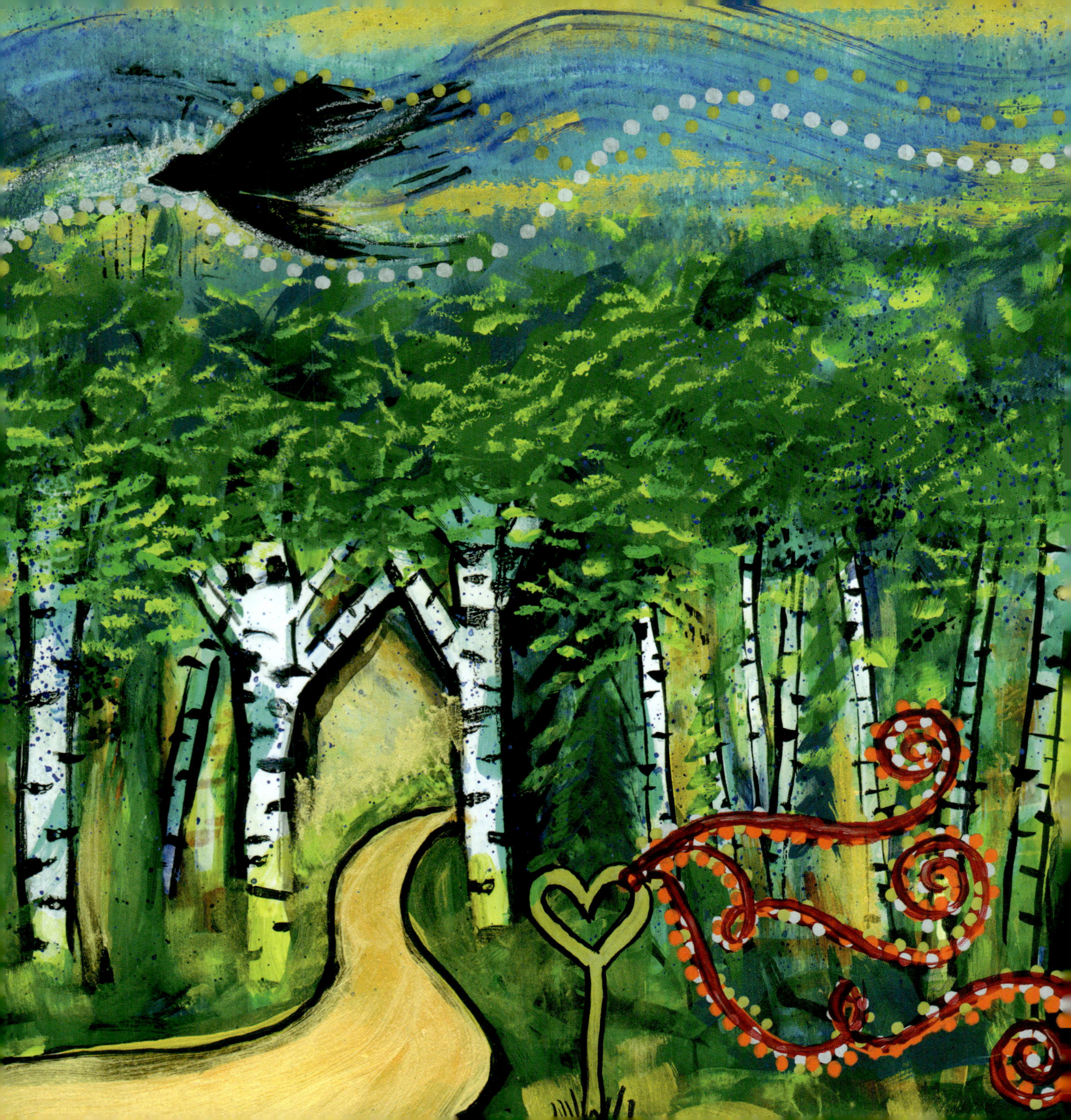

As you journey through life,
your address may change,
but the treasures inside will
always remain.

Questions

1. WHAT IS YOUR DEFINITION OF HOME?

2. ARE YOU OPEN TO EMBARKING ON A PERSONAL JOURNEY? WHAT DO YOU NEED TO PACK?

3. HOW WOULD YOU FEEL ABOUT STARTING A JOURNEY WITHOUT A MAP OR TIMETABLE BUT KNOWING YOU'LL ARRIVE AT A BEAUTIFUL DESTINATION? WHAT WOULD BE THE OBSTACLES? HOW MIGHT YOU BEST OVERCOME THEM?

4. ARE THERE RECURRING THEMES, DREAMS, OR IMAGES IN YOUR LIFE? IF SO, WRITE THEM DOWN AND KEEP YOUR EYES AND HEART OPEN FOR MORE. THESE ARE IMPORTANT!

5. HAVE YOU EVER CONSIDERED THAT THINGS IN NATURE MAY BE GIVING YOU A SIGN OR A MESSAGE? PERHAPS A PERFECTLY TIMED AND PLACED BIRD, FEATHER, OR RAINBOW?

6. CAN YOU NAME SOME TIMES IN YOUR LIFE WHERE YOU HAVE BEEN AWARE THAT YOUR INTUITION OR INNER KNOWING WAS GUIDING YOU?

7. DO YOU HAVE AN IDEA OF WHAT THE DOOR TO YOUR HEART MIGHT LOOK LIKE?

8. ONCE INSIDE, LOOK AROUND! WHAT DO SEE HERE? TAKE SOME TIME TO WRITE DOWN WHAT THIS SACRED SPACE LOOKS LIKE. IF YOU LISTEN CLOSELY, CAN YOU HEAR SOME WORDS THAT YOU KNOW ARE FOR YOU?

9. COULD YOU LET YOURSELF GET SO COMFORTABLE HERE THAT YOU COULD CALL IT YOUR HEART'S HOME?

Your Heart's Address

Whispers from Your Heart's Home

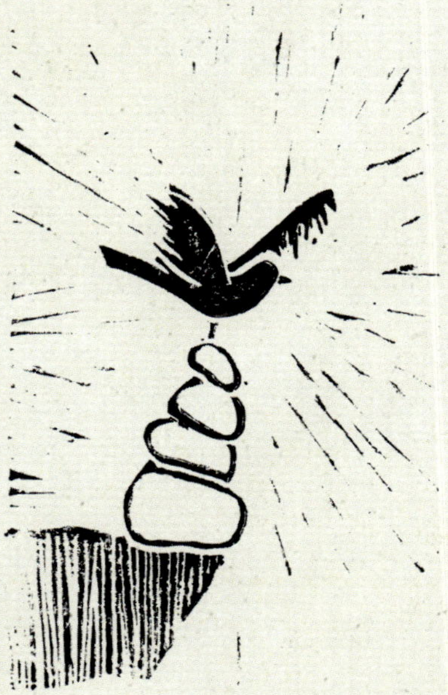

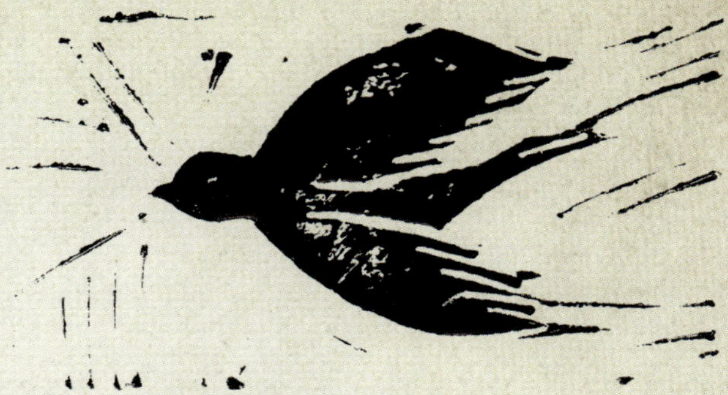

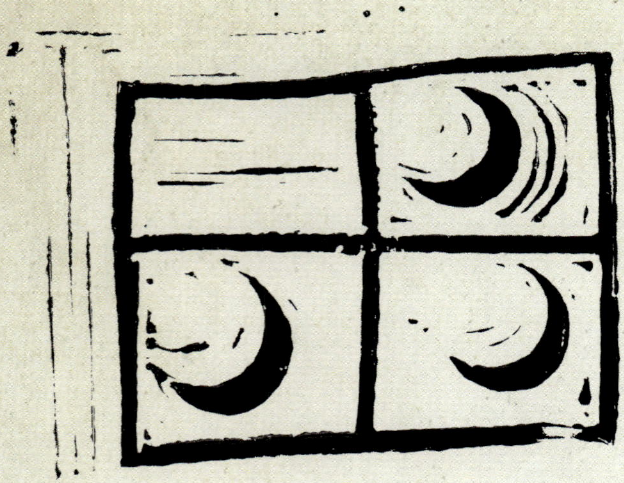

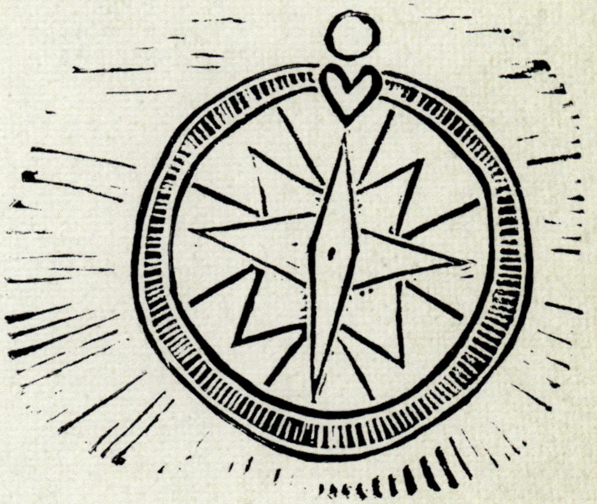

Acknowledgments

Along every mapped and unmapped journey there is delight when coming upon a cairn. A cairn is a trail marker that signifies you are on the right path, moving in the right direction. My work along the path was difficult at times, but the sharing of the lessons seemed easy and fell into place almost seamlessly. I would like to acknowledge the people who stood out to me as cairns as I traveled the unfamiliar territory of bringing my personal journey to print. It seemed these cairns were perfectly placed and I had true delight as I came upon each one.

What a joy meeting Amy Quale from Wise Ink Creative Publishing. We connected quickly and in a deep way. I saw in her eyes she understood the tears in mine as I vulnerably shared my story. Amy encouraged me to bring this story to life. She worked with me sharing her time and talent. Without her, the story would be untold.

Ara, my beautiful and gifted illustrator was, without a doubt, sent from above. I don't believe anybody could have captured this quite like she did. We are forever connected! Emily Rodvold, my book designer, so willing helped give birth to this book while at the same time giving birth to her own first born son!

Mary Kay Hoffman, my sister-in-law, friend, a skilled English teacher, and social media guru, listened carefully, steered me wisely, and dared to dream big with me.

Dear friends, all cairns of love and encouragement: Susi Eggeberger; Maxine Bergh; Eileen Massie; Lisa Michaux, a friend and book author; Sherry Essens; Jodi Peltier, a fellow dreamer and business partner; Brenda Williams, friend, artist, and creator of All Things

W'ren logo; and all the lovely yoga teachers from the Yellow Barn.

I am abundantly blessed with nine siblings, their spouses, and thirty-two nieces and nephews, all of whom share their love with me and are beacons of light.

My parents were true role models of love and sacrifice.

To my kids and their spouses, who maybe without knowing it have always made me curious to take this journey, knowing there was something more. I hope that this "something more" is passed down to you. I love you more than you'll ever know.

To Tom, with whom I share the backpack: You've encouraged and supported me in so many ways to continue to grow. That's what love does. . . .

And to Leni Erickson, a wise and loving guide, who held space for me these last few years. You encouraged me to trust my internal compass and helped me to remember so much. For this I will be forever grateful.

About the Author

Babs Fee and her husband have four children, three of whom are married, and six grand blessings. She grew up in Saint Paul, Minnesota and is the oldest daughter of ten children. From an early age, Babs actively listened and passionately pursued the journey of self discovery, and she continues to grow and develop through the practices of prayer, meditation, exercise, nutrition, and study. Babs attended St. Mary's School of Nursing. Upon graduation, she worked as a cardiac care and neonatal intensive care nurse. She is a certified yoga instructor through Kripalu School of Yoga and founded Yellow Barn Wellness. She is a co-founder of All Things W'ren. Babs renews herself by spending time with her family; she also enjoys reading, golf, tennis, hiking, cooking, and entertaining. Learn more at allthingswren.com.

About the Illustrator

Ara Elizabeth's art, like her life, explores the line between nature and fantasy, between the secret lives of animals and the poetry of flowers, between the imagination of children and the promise of independence. She lives in a cabin in the city, has more pets than she has children, and spends her days outdoors and her nights in her studio.